I Can Make My World a Safer Place

In Memory

of

Ruth Banks

Dedication

To all the kids we've lived with, worked with, and learned from

Ordering

Trade bookstores in the U.S. and Canada, please contact:

Publishers Group West
1700 Fourth Street, Berkeley CA 94710
Phone: (800) 788-3123   Fax: (510) 528-3444

Individuals can order our books from most bookstores or by calling toll-free:

(800) 266-5592

Hunter House books are available at bulk discounts for textbook course adoptions; to qualifying community, health care, and government organizations; and for special promotions and fund-raising. For details please contact:

Special Sales Department
Hunter House Inc.
PO Box 2914, Alameda CA 94501-0914
Phone: (510) 865-5282   Fax: (510) 865-4295
E-mail: ordering@hunterhouse.com

I Can Make My World

a Safer Place

A Kid's [...] Violence

Copyright © 2001 by Paul Kivel

Library of Congress Cataloging-in-Publication Data

Kivel, Paul.
  I can make my world a safer place: a kid's book about stopping violence / Paul Kivel; illustrated by Nancy Gorrell.--1st ed.
       p. cm.
  Includes bibliographical references.
  ISBN 0-89793-291-9 (pbk.)
  1. Violence--United States--Prevention--Juvenile literature. 2. Peace--Juvenile literature. [1. Violence. 2. Peace.] I. Gorrell, Nancy, ill. II. Title.
  HN79.V53 K58 2000
  303.6--dc21   00-063212

Project Credits

Cover Design: Virginia Fontana
Book Production: Hunter House and *osprey*design
Developmental Editor: David Ross McIrvine
Copy Editor: Barbara Keely
Proofreader: Melissa Millar
Graphics Coordinator: Ariel Parker
Acquisitions Editor: Jeanne Brondino
Associate Editor: Alexandra Mummery
Editorial & Production Assistant: Melissa Millar
Editorial Intern: Martha Benco
Publicity Manager: Sarah Frederick
Marketing Assistant: Earlita Chenault
Customer Service Manager: Christina Sverdrup
Order Fulfillment: Joel Irons
Administrator: Theresa Nelson
Publisher: Kiran S. Rana

Printed and bound by Publishers Press, Salt Lake City, Utah

Manufactured in the United States of America

9 8 7 6 5 4 3 2 1   First Edition   01 02 03 04 05

Table of Contents

A WORD OF WELCOME FROM THE AUTHOR

Why I Wrote This Book

I wrote this book to answer some of the questions you may have about what violence is and how to stop it. This book will give you lots of ideas about things to do. I hope you will use the ideas in this book to make it safer in your family, in your school, and in your neighborhood.

What This Book Is About

In this book I talk about many ways that a person might try to hurt the people around them or themselves, such as fights, family violence, gangs, bullies, and suicide. Each section has questions you can ask yourself, games, and suggestions for things you can do to make yourself and your world safer.

Ask Questions

You can read the book by yourself or you can ask someone older to read it to you. Stop reading at any time to think about what you are learning. Ask questions and talk with your friends and family. Violence is complicated, and people have many different experiences, thoughts, and feelings about it. No one person has all the answers but, when we put everyone's ideas together, we can come up with good solutions to the problem of violence.

Get Involved

The most important thing is that we do something to stop the violence and make it safer for everyone. Just recently more than one million people, many of them children, marched in the Million Moms March in cities across the country to demand safety locks on guns and better control over who can buy guns. Other people are working for less violence on TV, for conflict resolution programs in schools, and for aid to victims of violence. There are people everywhere who are doing things to make it safer. You can be one of them.

Join Us

Join with me and many other children and adults to make the peace. We each have a role to play and together we can make a difference. P.S. This is an activity book. However, before you write in the book check with a parent or teacher to make sure it's okay. If it isn't, you can write the answers to the games on a separate sheet of paper.

For Parents, Teachers, and Other Adults

I wrote this book to give children an opportunity to talk about the kinds of violence that they see or hear about, or possibly experience, in our society. It can also provide you with an opportunity to raise issues of violence in a non-threatening, interactive manner. Whether read alone or with an adult, the book can help dispel children's fears, correct misinformation, and provide them with positive ways to become involved in community efforts to stop the violence and make the peace.

As a parent and educator, I know that young people are often more ready to talk about these issues, and more exposed to them, than most adults imagine. In addition, it may not be easy for us to raise the subject of violence with our children because of our own experiences, fears, and uncertainty. I hope this book will be useful for you in addressing these difficult issues. You may also want to talk with other adults or do some reading on your own beforehand to better prepare you.[1]

The most difficult challenge for me as a parent and teacher has been to learn how to really listen to what children are saying. I don't find it easy to fully acknowledge their questions, fears, thoughts, and feelings without overlaying my own opinions and judgments. I encourage you to use this book as an opportunity, not just to teach children about violence, but also to open up a space for them to explore, to think and share feelings about, and to become involved in the complex and often confusing world around them.

We know that children have a deep sense of caring about others and a passion for fairness ("It's not fair!" is one of their favorite expressions). With our support, they can become active in community efforts to make the world less violent, safer, and more just.

NOTE: Children who have been traumatized by violence that has happened to them, to those around them, or in their immediate communities need personal counseling. If you think a child you are working with has experienced violent trauma, consult with a counselor or therapist for recommendations and advice. This book cannot substitute for professional intervention.

[1] A good book to start with is *Talking with Your Child About A Troubled World* by Lynne S. Dumas, New York: Fawcett Columbine, 1992.

Chapter 1

It's Okay to Be Angry

Anger is a normal feeling that people have when they are hurt or frustrated or don't get what they want. But anger can be a scary feeling because some people get violent when they get angry.

It's okay to be angry. It's not okay to hurt someone because you are angry. Stopping the cycle of violence means breaking the connection between anger and violence.

Anger Doesn't Make Us Violent

When we get angry, we can decide what to do. Instead of yelling or hitting, we can talk about the problem, run around the block, draw a picture, or hit a pillow.

When I get angry I usually

_____

_____

_____

_____

When my parent(s) get angry they usually

_____

_____

_____

_____

DRAW SOMETHING THAT MAKES YOU ANGRY

Things to do

Instead of yelling run around the block.

Instead of hitting draw how you feel.

Make a list of different things you can do when you get angry that don't involve hurting someone.

When I get angry I can

_____

_____

_____

_____

_____

We are usually angry because...

Something is wrong.

Something is not the way we want it to be.

When you get angry, you can think about what it is you want to change.
Then you can decide what to do about it.
Your anger can guide you to finding the **right** solution.

Make an Anger Checklist

Something that makes me angry **What I can do about it**

1. _____   _____

2. _____   _____

3. _____   _____

4. _____   _____

5. _____   _____

Four People Who Used Their Anger in a Good Way

Dr. Martin Luther King Jr. was angry because black people were being treated unfairly. He was a minister who led people in the United States to strike, boycott, and march together so that laws that were unfair to African Americans would be changed.

Julia Butterfly Hill was angry because logging companies were cutting down ancient redwood trees. Julia lived in an old redwood tree for two years to protect it from being cut down. Only when the logging company said it would not cut down her tree and would protect the area around it did she agree to come down.

Harriet Tubman was angry about slavery. Harriet escaped from slavery in the South to freedom in the North. She returned to the South many times to rescue her relatives and other slaves on the Underground Railroad.

César Chavez was angry at the low pay and bad working conditions that big farming companies forced on farmworkers. He started the United Farmworkers Union and led farmworkers in strikes to get higher wages and better working conditions.

Draw a line to the correct name

A. Protested to get higher wages for farmworkers

B. Lived in an ancient redwood tree to save it

C. Escaped from slavery and led others out, too

D. Organized people to get laws changed for equal rights

1. Julia Butterfly Hill

2. Harriet Tubman

3. Dr. Martin Luther King, Jr.

4. César Chavez

Answers: A = 4 B = 1 C = 2 D = 3

Chapter 2

Leaders and Bullies

- Everyone can be a leader.
- A real leader is not violent.
- Leaders use communication and courage to lead others.
- A true leader thinks of what is best for the whole group.

A leader uses COOPERATIVE POWER...

Cooperative power comes from people working together. What are some things that people can do when they work together?

...and then there are BULLIES.

Bullies try to make others do what they want by threatening and hurting them.

Bullies want people to be afraid and to do what the bully wants out of fear.

Bullies...

scare and hurt other people. However—they may look strong on the outside, but inside they often feel scared and bad about themselves.

Why Do Bullies Pick on People?

Bullies usually don't feel good about themselves.

They try to find something different about other people and take advantage of it.

Some differences bullies use to pick on people are:

- Race
- Religion
- Family Lifestyle
- Size
- Physical Ability
- Male/Female Differences

There are many differences among people, and each person is one-of-a-kind. If we were all the same it would be a

DULL, BORING WORLD

Bully Power Hurts Everyone

Bully power comes from being bigger, stronger, or having more people, money, or weapons on your side. Bully power only makes people angry. It makes them not want to do anything for the bully.

Have you ever been a bully?

It's not a good idea to be a bully because it hurts others and yourself.

You may get caught by parents, a teacher, or even the police.

You might meet a bigger bully who is stronger or more violent than you are.

Things to do if you are a bully...

A Crossword Puzzle

Bullies build walls of bad feelings.
Kids don't like or trust them.

ACROSS

1. A bully can be _ _ _ _ or killed if someone fights back.
2. A bully knows he or she is doing wrong, so may feel _ _ _ _ _ _.
3. A bully may feel _ _ _ _ _ _ because he or she may be caught.

DOWN

4. A bully feels _ _ _ _ _ and takes it out on people.
5. It is _ _ _ _ _ _ _ _ _ to be a bully.
6. After a bully hurts someone, he or she can feel _ _ _ _ _ _ _.
7. A bully doesn't have many _ _ _ _ _ _ _.
8. A bully _ _ _ _ _ on smaller or younger people.

WORD LIST: GUILTY, ANGRY, DANGEROUS, FRIENDS, PICKS, HURT, SCARED, ASHAMED

Chapter 3

Fights

Name-calling, teasing, pushing and shoving, and threats can all lead to fights. Fights can also start when two people want the same thing at the same time, like a book or a ball. These kinds of fights are usually unnecessary. There are many ways to solve a problem without fighting.

Avoid Escalation . . . Try Understanding (Empathy)

Getting into a fight can feel like being on an escalator that you can't stop—even if you change your mind. You just keep getting angrier and angrier. But you can stop fights by taking a deep breath and asking yourself what's going on. What else could you be doing besides fighting?

I UNDERSTAND YOU ARE GOING THROUGH A HARD TIME.

Empathy means trying to understand and feel what someone else is feeling. Try to put yourself in someone else's place and you can better understand why they said or did something that made you angry or hurt your feelings.

Things to do if there is a fight between your friends...

Unscramble

Don't just watch—help problem solve. Unscramble words from the pictures below that can make it safer.

N!LSET TO BOTH SIDES.

HELP EACH NOPSER TO LISTEN TO EACH OTHER.

ASK AN LUTAD TO HELP.

WHY YOU... ⊙!©☆! ASK EACH PERSON NOT TO CALL EMANS.

I NEED YOU TO... IT WOULD BE OK IF.. ASK THEM TO SAY WHAT THEY TAWN.

HELP THINK OF ASIDE TO HELP SOLVE THE PROBLEM.

Some ideas for problem solving

On the way to the park, Malcolm and David started to fight. Tenisha asked them to stop fighting and start talking. She listened to them while they explained how they felt.

By the time they got to the park, they had solved their problem. Can you follow the path they took to get to the park? Avoid the traps and use the safe path.

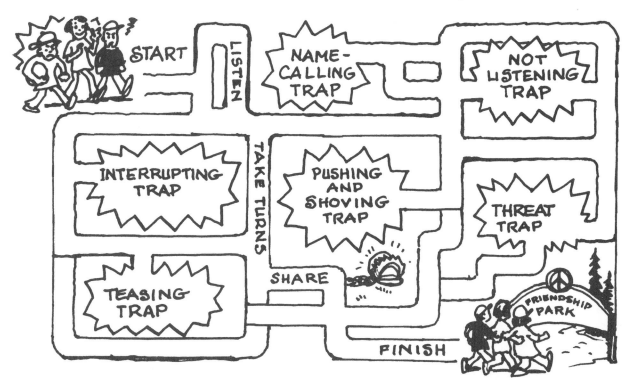

START

LISTEN

NAME-CALLING TRAP

NOT LISTENING TRAP

INTERRUPTING TRAP

TAKE TURNS

PUSHING AND SHOVING TRAP

THREAT TRAP

TEASING TRAP

SHARE

FRIENDSHIP PARK

FINISH

23

Chapter 4

TV, Movies, Games, and Play

You can see a lot of bullying, fights, teasing, and name-calling on TV and in the movies. This is called media violence. When you watch media violence you might begin to think that it's okay to use violence to solve problems or to get people to do things.

The violence on TV and in movies is made to seem real, but it's just pretend. Real violence means that people may get killed and may never talk or eat or have friends again. In real violence innocent people who are walking or standing nearby can get hurt.

HOW WOULD IT FEEL IF THE PEOPLE GETTING HURT ON TV WERE PEOPLE YOU KNEW?

POW! BAM!

The more violence you watch on TV or in movies, the more likely you are to be violent later on. Watching violence doesn't cause you to be violent. However, it does give you the idea that violence is a good way to solve problems and is not too dangerous.

LIST TV SHOWS THAT SHOW VIOLENCE:

1 _____
2 _____
3 _____
4 _____
5 _____

LIST SHOWS THAT SHOW PEOPLE LIVING TOGETHER WITHOUT VIOLENCE:

1 _____
2 _____
3 _____
4 _____
5 _____

Scary TV

Watching violence on television, whether it's in movies, regular programs, or even on the news, can also make you more afraid of being hurt by other people. This might give you nightmares or dreams that frighten you. It might make you scared to be by yourself. It could make you think about getting a weapon to protect yourself. Did you ever see a scary movie and then feel afraid afterwards? Did you ever have nightmares about things you saw on television or in a movie?

UNSCRAMBLE THESE SCARY
TV OR MOVIE WORDS:

CRAY S

O S E TRN M

OBOLD

Answers: 1. Scary 2. Monster 3. Blood

Things to do

Other things you can do: _____

_____ _____

_____ _____

_____ _____

Reading about Violence

Because there is so much violence described in the newspapers, it's normal for young people to have fears and nightmares about violence. Sometimes you may be afraid or dream that it will happen to you or to your family and friends. Remind yourself that your dreams are not real, and violence probably won't actually happen to you.

Things to do if you worry or dream about violence...

Talk about your fears and dreams with adults around you.

Think about what you can do in real situations where you feel scared, such as being home alone, and make plans.

Tell yourself that it's only a dream or a worry. It's okay to have them, but they won't make violence happen to you.

Violent Toys

There are a lot of toys sold for young people that have guns or other weapons for killing. Many video games also have people shooting or hurting other people. Toys are not real, but they do give you pretend practice in hurting people. If you play with guns or games that are violent, you are learning that it's okay to hurt people rather than help them, to shoot them rather than talk with them. This might make it more likely that you use violence or that you use a weapon to hurt someone when you are older. Are there any toys or video games you play with that pretend people are killing other people?

List toys or video games that use violence:

_____

_____

_____

_____

_____

_____

_____

Things to do

- Buy toys that allow you to create things, solve problems, or be cooperative.
- Don't buy toys and games or other products that are violent.
- Write letters to the companies that make violent toys and games and tell them why you won't buy them.
- Talk with other young people about not buying those things.

Chapter 5

More about Violence

Violence is:

Violence Hurts

Violence hurts our bodies, our minds, and our feelings. A person may be hurt so badly that they have to go to a hospital.

Violence hurts the families, friends, and communities of those killed, too.

Afterwards, people who have been hurt may be afraid of being attacked again.

They may feel angry at the person who hurt them.

They may feel sad, confused, embarrassed, powerless, or want to hurt someone else to get even.

It can take a long time to heal from violence.

Do you know someone who was hurt badly or killed by an act of violence?

Did it scare you?

Did you feel sad, angry, or confused?

Did you feel afraid that you might be hurt, too?

These feelings are normal.

You probably have a lot of questions about what happened and how and why.

You have a right to know, but you may have to wait until that person is less upset to ask about it.

It's important to talk about your feelings.

When someone is killed by an act of violence, you may wonder why was it that person instead of someone else. No one knows why some people are hurt or killed by violence.

Often there doesn't seem to be any reason why it was that particular person. One of the hardest things to understand about violence is why some people get hurt or attacked and others don't.

DRAW A PICTURE OF SOMETHING VIOLENT THAT YOU HAVE SEEN OR HEARD ABOUT

Fill in the lines between the dots to find out who is **not** violent.

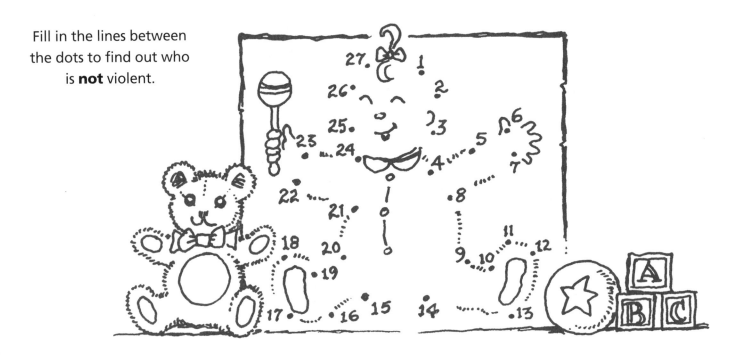

Most scientists agree that babies aren't born violent. We do know that young people learn to be violent from the people, especially the adults, around them.

In countries where there is little violence, the children grow up and aren't violent. In countries like ours where there is lots of violence, the children grow up and learn to be violent.

When we are hurt, sometimes we find someone else to hurt because we think it may make us feel better.

For example, if your dad hurts you, you may be very angry with him. You probably wouldn't hit him back because he is bigger than you, so you might go and hurt your little brother or sister instead. This produces a cycle of violence where violence leads to more violence.

The *cycle of violence* is dangerous because it goes on and on and more people get hurt. Did you ever hurt someone smaller than you because you were feeling angry and upset?

Many of us are caught in the cycle of violence—when we have been hurt by violence.

Have you ever been: **By whom?**

hit?   ___ yes   ___ no   _____

slapped?   ___ yes   ___ no   _____

kicked?   ___ yes   ___ no   _____

teased?   ___ yes   ___ no   _____

called names?   ___ yes   ___ no   _____

kissed or touched in a ___ yes   ___ no   _____
   way that upset
   or scared you?

VIOLENCE CHECK ✓

(continued)

And some of us have hurt others...

Have you ever:			**Who?**
hit someone?	___ yes	___ no	_____
slapped someone?	___ yes	___ no	_____
kicked someone?	___ yes	___ no	_____
teased someone?	___ yes	___ no	_____
called someone names?	___ yes	___ no	_____
kissed or touched someone in a way that upset or scared him or her?	___ yes	___ no	_____

What Helps?

Many times problem solving can prevent violence, but not always. Sometimes if we are attacked, we may not even know why. Someone else was hurt and in pain, and they turned their pain into anger and their anger into violence against you. It's not your fault if someone has been or is violent with you. You didn't ask to be hurt. Nobody deserves to be hurt, no matter what they do.

TALKING TO OTHERS CAN HELP.

♡ FRIENDS CLINIC ♡ ♡

WHAT CAN I DO FOR YOU?

IT CAN TAKE A LONG TIME TO HEAL FROM VIOLENCE

Chapter 6

Three Kinds of Violence

Bullies use three kinds of violence to get what they want:

- Physical Violence
- Sexual Violence
- Emotional Violence

Physical Violence

Hitting, kicking, slapping, punching, biting, and throwing things at someone are all examples of **physical violence.** Taking something away from someone or making them do something they don't want to do can also be a kind of violence.

Physical violence is also called bullying, assault, or battery. Have you ever been hurt by physical violence? What happened? How did you feel?

One time I was hurt was

_____

This is what happened

_____

_____

_____

_____

I felt

_____

_____

_____

_____

Things to do if you are the person getting hurt...

Talk to someone about it.

Get help from your friends or from someone you trust.

Things to do if there is a fight or someone else is getting hurt...

Emotional Violence

STUPID!

MEAN WORDS THAT HURT...

You can also hurt someone with words. Yelling, teasing, calling names, saying you're going to break things or hit someone if they don't do what you want are all kinds of emotional violence.

Words like "stupid," "sissy," or "wimp" hurt us and make us feel attacked. They are violent even if the person who says them says, "It's just a joke," or "I didn't really mean it."

List any words that you hear or know that hurt people:

_____

_____

_____

_____

_____

Things to do

- Don't tease.
- If you or anyone else is being teased, tell the person doing the teasing that you don't like it and want him or her to stop.
- Treat everyone with respect.
- Talk with your friends and family about how words can hurt people.

If Looks Could Kill . . . (hurting feelings)

Sometimes mean words can hurt as much as hitting. Sometimes it's not just the words, but an action or look that hurts. Circle the things that can hurt:

LOCKING OUT

DIRTY LOOKS

HONESTY

PUT-DOWNS

JOKING

IGNORING

SHARING

GOSSIP

TALKING BEHIND SOMEONE'S BACK

DITCHING SOMEONE

PRETENDING TO BE A FRIEND TO GET SOMETHING

Draw a line from a hurtful thing in the first group to a better thing to do in the second group:

laughing at someone

locking out from a game

silent treatment when angry

gossiping and spreading rumors

talking behind a person's back

use your words to express how you feel

include everyone and take turns

laughing with someone

talk directly to the person in an honest way

don't say anything about someone if you don't know if it is true

Sexual Violence

Touching, kissing, or hugging someone when he or she doesn't want to be, or making someone do something sexual he or she doesn't want to do can be violence if a person is hurt or feels scared or attacked.

Other words for sexual violence are rape, sexual assault, molestation, or incest. Sexual violence can happen to both boys and girls.

 ## Things to do if you are sexually assaulted...

TALK TO SOMEONE ABOUT IT

GET HELP

REMEMBER, IT ISN'T YOUR FAULT

Things to do if someone else is being sexually assaulted...

LET THEM KNOW YOU CARE.

TELL AN ADULT YOU TRUST.

Search-a-Word

Search for the words that will help when there has been a fight or sexual assault.

Example: It is important to T A L K to someone about it.

```
T I S N V X B C R A T F L T
T H U R T F S C A R E R A Z
O A L S R W A N O G H I P D
V A L K U Y D U C J L E R M
G S A K S R H M L Y O N K L
B O W A T C H V E T R D Z B
```

Don't stand around and **W** _ _ _ _.

Help the person who is **H** _ _ _.

Tell an adult you **T** _ _ _ _.

Be a **F** _ _ _ _ _. Let the hurt person know you **C** _ _ _.

Remember, it isn't your **F** _ _ _ _.

52

Words: TRUST, CARE, FRIEND, HURT, WATCH, FAULT

Chapter 7

Private Danger

Violence at Home, Drugs, Hurting Yourself

Private danger is when you are hurt by someone you know such as a neighbor, teacher, friend, parent, or other relative. If your parents hit you or a relative sexually molests you—these are private dangers.

Private dangers can be hard to talk about. If you are in private danger it is important to get help. Is there any private danger that makes you feel unsafe?

Sometimes even our own families can feel scary and dangerous. It can feel like a war where everyone is fighting and hurting each other, or where one person is bullying everyone else. At other times our families can seem very peaceful, but one person may be hurting another person without other family members knowing about it.

OW! STOP! I DON'T WANT YOU TO DO THAT!

Things to do if you are unsafe or another family member is unsafe...

IF YOU ARE BEING HURT BY A FAMILY MEMBER, TELL A PARENT, RELATIVE, OR FRIEND ABOUT IT.

IF ANOTHER MEMBER OF YOUR FAMILY IS BEING HURT, TALK WITH THEM. SUPPORT THEIR GETTING HELP.

Domestic Violence

When one adult hits or hurts another adult in a family it is called domestic violence. Domestic violence is very scary and very dangerous. Sometimes only an adult is hurt, but sometimes the children are hurt, too.

Even if the children are not being hurt directly, they may feel scared, confused, angry, or upset. They may think that they did something to cause the violence.

Remember that only the bully is responsible for the violence, not you or anyone else around.

Things to do if there is domestic violence in your family...

STAY OUT OF THE WAY AS MUCH AS YOU CAN.

TALK TO YOUR BROTHERS & SISTERS IF YOU HAVE ANY.

TALK TO YOUR PARENTS ABOUT HOW THE VIOLENCE MAKES YOU FEEL.

TALK TO SOMEONE ELSE ABOUT WHAT IS GOING ON IN YOUR FAMILY.

A RELATIVE   A GOOD FRIEND

A TEACHER OR CHILD CARE PROVIDER

It's not your fault if there is violence in your family. Adults may use bully power to hit, yell, scream, throw things at, or hurt another adult for reasons that have nothing to do with the children.

Drugs in the Family

If someone in a family is using a lot of drugs and acting mean or violent, it can be dangerous for the rest of the family. Drugs don't cause violence, but people who are violent often use drugs.

  ## Things to do

If a family member uses drugs, talk to someone you trust such as a relative or neighbor about getting help for your family member.

Hurting Yourself

Instead of hurting others, some people try to hurt themselves when they are feeling scared, hurt, lonely, or angry. They might use drugs to try to feel better. They might do something very dangerous to try to kill themselves.

This is called suicide. These people forget that things can get better. They can get help, find friends, and lead long and good lives. It's just as useless to hurt oneself as it is to hurt someone else.

WE FORGET THAT THINGS CAN GET BETTER

Things to do if you feel like hurting yourself...

Stop and think about what is bothering you. Talk to someone about it. Remember that hurting yourself is not going to make anything better. You are an important person and the world will miss you.

WITHOUT YOU...

WITH YOU...

If you hear a friend or family member talk about hurting or killing himself or herself, tell that person you don't want them to and you would miss them. Tell someone you trust, such as a parent or teacher, that your friend has talked about hurting himself or herself.

Using drugs can also be a way to hurt yourself. Drugs can:

- make you sick
- make you sick slowly so that you won't live as long as other people
- make you have accidents
- kill you

Some common drugs are: cigarettes, chewing tobacco, alcohol, cocaine, marijuana, heroin, speed, methamphetamines, crack, and PCP.

For more about drugs, see page 70

Chapter 8

Public Danger

Crime, Weapons, Gangs, and War

Most people don't talk about private danger, but they do talk about public danger. Public danger comes from being in a public place where violence is happening.

Some examples are being kidnapped by a stranger, being robbed at home or in the street, being shot, or hit in a fight at school or in the street.

Often young people are told about public dangers and what to do to protect themselves. "Don't talk to strangers" is one thing that adults tell young people about public danger.

Are there any public dangers that you worry about?

Draw a picture of Public Danger

Things to do if you face public danger...

Weapons

Weapons such as knives and guns make fights more dangerous. The only purpose weapons have is to hurt people.

You may think you can use a weapon to protect yourself, but using or just having a knife or gun is likely to make it more dangerous for you and others. Every year many children die from accidents with guns. What can be dangerous about having a weapon?

Find the hidden pictures where great danger lurks...find 5 knives, 5 guns, and 2 chains.

Things to do if you see a knife or gun...

- Avoid knives, guns, and people who carry them.

- If you notice someone with a weapon at school, tell a teacher or other adult.

- Never assume that a knife isn't sharp or that a gun isn't loaded.

- Never point a weapon at anyone, even in fun.

Things to do for a safer community...

- Don't play with toy guns or pretend weapons.
- Play cooperative games.
- Talk to your parents about gun safety and gun locks.
- Get together with other people who are concerned about gun safety.

Little Wars

Sometimes there are little wars on our streets and in our neighborhoods. There are no bombs or tanks in these wars, but people (usually men) do use guns and other weapons.

When one group of people is fighting another group for drugs or to control a neighborhood, or when the neighbors and the police are fighting, it can be like being in a war. It is dangerous. People get killed or hurt and everyone is scared.

Do you ever feel like there is a war going on in your neighborhood?

Are there gangs in your neighborhood?

It's good that people come together in groups, in teams and clubs, and to work with others. A gang is a group that comes together to hurt people. Sometimes people join gangs to have friends, to stay safe, or to hurt others.

Gangs may make the members feel powerful, but they make a neighborhood very unsafe for everyone else. People in gangs can even hurt each other and make their members do things they don't really want to do just to be part of the gang.

GANGS FOLLOW LIKE SHEEP.

 Things to do

- Only be part of groups that don't involve hurting people.
- Talk to your parents or someone you trust if you are being pressured to join a gang.
- Get involved in a club, after-school arts, or a sports program.

Drugs

Drugs can also contribute to public danger because people fight to get drugs that are illegal (against the law) and to get money to buy these drugs. People even kill each other to buy illegal drugs or to get money for drugs.

Sometimes people who are nearby get hurt or killed because of drug fighting. There are people who use drugs in every neighborhood. In some neighborhoods, people use drugs quietly and don't get much attention. In other neighborhoods, drug use is more visible to others.

Do you know anyone who uses drugs?

Things to do to stay safe from drugs...

War

War is another kind of public danger where one group of people attacks another group with guns and big weapons like tanks.

Many, many people get killed and wounded in a war. Many other living things and communities are destroyed. Houses, farms, and factories are damaged and often there is great harm to animals, plants, and the natural environment that can last for years.

Sometimes people fight a war to defend themselves when they are attacked or to win their freedom. But most of the time, wars, like other kinds of violence, are avoidable.

Chapter 9

Getting Help, Fighting Back, and Running Away

It's always a good idea to try and find help when violence is happening. Some people to go to for help are:

- your parents
- other relatives
- friends and neighbors
- teachers
- the police—just call 911

 Things to do

List at least two people you can talk with if you need to get help. People I can talk to:

_____

_____

Talking with Adults about Violence

It's always okay to talk about violence when it happens to you or around you.

Sometimes, if someone is hurting you, they will tell you that if you tell anyone they will hurt you more or hurt someone in your family. They are trying to make you too scared to get help. But it's even more important that you try to get help so that person will stop hurting you.

THREATS IF YOU TELL

NOT LISTENING

I UNDERSTAND. I BELIEVE YOU!

KEEP TRYING! DEALING WITH VIOLENCE CAN FEEL LIKE CLIMBING A MOUNTAIN.

If you tell an adult about violence that is happening and he or she doesn't believe you, you may have to tell someone else. Keep trying, because you deserve to get help.

Avoiding Violence is Important

When violence is happening, it's always okay to leave to protect yourself. If it's possible, you should go get help. Stay safe yourself.

Some boys think that it's not okay to run away from a fight or other danger. That is silly. Avoiding violence is important.

Things to do

Make a list of safe places you can go when there is violence happening around you.

For example, if there is violence at home, maybe you can go to your room, to a friend's house, to an aunt's, or to your grandparents' house.

If there is danger at school, you can walk with friends, avoid certain areas of the school, or go to the counselor's office.

Safe places I can go when there is violence around me:

At home:

_____
_____
_____

At school:

_____
_____
_____

In the neighborhood:

_____
_____
_____

Draw a picture of one of these places

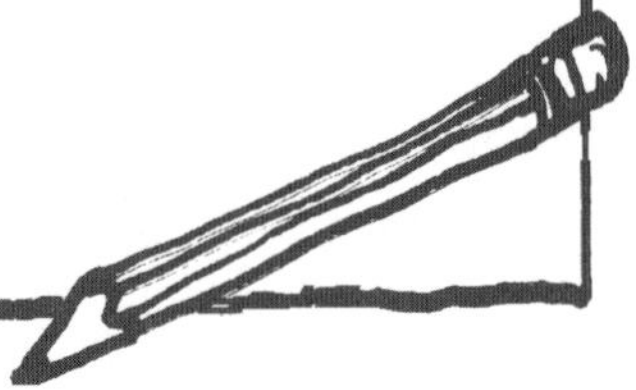

Fighting Back

Sometimes, if you or someone around you is getting hurt you might want to fight back or help. Be very careful. Even if you are strong you may end up being one more person who gets hurt.

It is often better to go and get help than to get into a fight.

YOU MIGHT END UP JUST ONE MORE PERSON GETTING HURT

Many boys think they should fight back or protect someone, such as their mother, who may be getting hurt, because they are "the guy."

Even if you are a strong boy and have some practice fighting, this is a very dangerous thing to do. You could get hurt or increase the violence. If the police were to come, they could lock you up for being violent even if you were just trying to help.

It's better to get help if you can or get more people to stop the violence.

 ## Things to do instead of fighting back...

YELL LOUDLY!   RUN FOR HELP...   CALL THE POLICE

Decode this secret message...

Running Away

Sometimes young people grow up in families or neighborhoods where there is violence and there isn't much that they can do to change things and make it safer. However, when they get bigger they can leave and get help and be in a safer place.

Many young people think about running away because they are being hurt at home or school.

Running away isn't easy. It can be very dangerous living on the streets. To live on your own, you need money and a place to stay or a person or family to live with.

RUNNING AWAY CAN BE DANGEROUS

Chapter 10

Let's Make the Peace

We can't get rid of violence by ourselves, but we can do it together with cooperative power.

Many young people and adults have already started working together to stop violence on TV, get rid of violent toys, make our neighborhoods safer, and stop war.

Get together with other young people and adults you know and decide what you are going to do to help stop the violence.

My Pledge

(solve the puzzle below for the first line of the pledge)

_ _   _ _ _ _ _   _ _ _ _   _ _ _ _   _ _ _ _ _ _ _

I WILL TRY NOT TO FIGHT

I WILL TRY TO MAKE THE PEACE

Signed _____

Date _____

What are you going to do?

STOP VIOLENCE ON TELEVISION

GET RID OF VIOLENT TOYS

MAKE OUR NEIGHBORHOODS SAFER

STOP WAR – USE WORDS, NOT WEAPONS

A crossword puzzle about Making the Peace

ACROSS

1. **J** _ _ _ _ _ _ a group which is not violent is a good thing to do.
2. When someone is hurt, go get **H** _ _ _.
3. Don't play with **G** _ _ _.
4. When violence is shown on _ _, turn it off.
5. To **E** _ _ _ _ _ _ _ things in a fight makes things worse.

DOWN

6. People can get more done if they **C** _ _ _ _ _ _ _ _.
7. A group that uses violence to get power is called a **G** _ _ _.
8. People who want to hurt themselves should remember that things can get B _ _ _ _ _.
9. Trying to understand what other people feel is called **E** _ _ _ _ _ _.
10. A person who helps people without using violence is a **L** _ _ _ _ _.

M A K E T H E P E A C E

(84)

Let's Review! ... a Fill-in-the-Blanks Game

Find the definitions of different kinds of violence from the word list:

When someone hits or kicks someone else, it is called **P**_____ violence.

When someone kisses or touches another person's body or makes him or her do something sexual he or she doesn't want to do, it is called **S**_____ violence.

When a group of young people come together to have power over others by threatening or hurting them, it is called **G**_____ violence.

When someone kills herself or himself on purpose, it is called **S**_____.

When someone uses names or other words to hurt a person, it is called **E**_____ violence.

When one country or large group of people attack another country or group of people, it is called **W**_____.

When there is violence on TV or in movies, it is called **M**_____ violence.

When one adult hurts another adult in a family, it is called **D**_____ violence.

A Word Puzzle

How many words can you make out of the letters in the phrase:

M A K E   T H E   P E A C E

Take, pea, eat, tack, math—can you think of others?

_____   _____   _____

_____   _____   _____

_____   _____   _____

_____   _____   _____

_____   _____   _____

_____   _____   _____

_____   _____   _____

You can make a lot by making the peace!

There are 11 differences between these pictures. Can you find them?

Other Books to Read

Berenstain Bears and the Bully by Stan and Jan Berenstain. New York: Random House, 1993.

Berenstain Bears and Too Much Teasing by Stan and Jan Berenstain. New York: Random House, 1995.

Berenstain Bears Get in a Fight by Stan and Jan Berenstain. New York: Random House, 1982.

The Boy Who Sat by the Window by Chris Loftis. Far Hills, NJ: New Horizon Press, 1996.

Bullies Are a Pain in the Brain by Trevor Romain. Minneapolis, MN: Free Spirit Publishing, 1997.

The Butter Battle Book by Dr. Seuss. New York: Random House, 1985.

Peace Tales: World Folktales to Talk About by Margaret R. MacDonald. Hamden, CT: Linnet Books, 1992.

Potatoes, Potatoes by Anita Lobel. New York: Harper and Row, 1967.

The Safe Zone: A Kid's Guide to Personal Safety by Donna Chaiet and Francine Russell. New York: Beech Tree Books, 1998.

The Sneetches and other Stories by Dr. Seuss (T. Giesel). New York: Random House, 1961.

The Story of Ferdinand by Leaf Munro. New York: Viking Press, 1936.

The Streets are Free by Kurusa. Toronto: Annick Press, 1985.

The Tomato Patch by William Wondriska. New York: Rinehart & Winston, 1964.

The Words Hurt by Chris Loftis. Far Hills, NJ: New Horizon Press, 1994.

Yertle the Turtle and other Stories by Dr. Seuss. New York: Random House, 1950, 1951, 1958.